Speaking With Signs

Children's Object Lessons
For Lent And Easter

Wesley T. Runk

CSS Publishing Company, Inc.
Lima, Ohio

2nd Edition
Copyright © 1975, 1995 by
CSS Publishing Company, Inc.
Lima, Ohio

Scripture quotations are from the *New Revised Standard Version of the Bible,* copyright 1989, by the Division of Christian Education of the National Council of the Churches of Christ in the USA. Used by permission.

ISBN 0-7880-0371-2

He who saw this has testified so that you also may believe.

— John 19:35a

Table Of Contents

The Lantern

So Judas brought a detachment of soldiers together with police from the chief priests and the Pharisees, and they came there with lanterns and torches and weapons.

— John 18:3

Object: A lantern

Good morning, boys and girls. Over the next couple of weeks I want to share some stories with you about some soldiers and a man whom they hardly knew named Jesus. The stories are exciting because they make us feel sad, afraid, courageous and happy. But remember, the stories that I am telling you really happened. Not one of them is make-believe. Each of these stories can be found in the Bible, and I am going to give you something each week so that you will always remember them.

Today's story begins in the temple where a group of priests and Pharisees were meeting to discuss some evil plans they had to get rid of Jesus. They did not want anyone else to know of their meeting except those who had to carry out the plan. For this reason they met late in the evening after it had become very dark. If you were watching from any distance you would have had a difficult time seeing the faces of the men who were planning. There were no electric lights or flashlights, but instead they had lanterns hanging in the corners to give just enough light to see but not enough to be seen.

When the meeting broke up in the very late hours, they sent for some soldiers who were stationed around the temple to guard it. Can you imagine having soldiers standing outside our church guarding it? I can't either. But that is where they were ordered to keep the night watch. One of the men who had been in the meeting approached the sergeant and told him what to do. He was to take a lantern or two and cross a valley to a certain spot in an olive grove and there arrest a certain man. The soldiers were told that this man was dangerous to the whole city of Jerusalem and an enemy of Rome.

Soldiers know that it is their responsibility to protect their country from dangerous people and these soldiers were no different than any others who have a job to do. There was one other thing about the mission that was different than other missions. The man they were looking for might not be alone. They were told to leave the others alone and just bring back the one who was considered dangerous, an enemy of the people. To make sure that they had the right man, the priests and Pharisees told them to follow another man, Judas, who was a former disciple of this dangerous man. He was to point out the one to be captured.

The soldiers took some lanterns from the temple, walked across the temple courtyard, through the city gate and down to the Kidron Valley. It was pitch black and hard to see with such little light. But Judas knew where he was going as he had been there many times with Jesus. When they finally arrived at the entrance to the olive grove, Judas told the men to light some torches, follow him and arrest the man he kissed on the side of the cheek. With lanterns glowing and torches blazing the soldiers rushed into the garden, prepared to fight this dangerous man and his army.

Judas went first with his arms open and politely gave Jesus a kiss on the cheek. The soldiers stood there with swords drawn and shields raised to face an unarmed Jesus and eleven other men who had just been wakened by the noise. One of the friends of Jesus jumped to his feet, grabbed a soldier's sword and cut off the ear of one of the soldiers. But Jesus stopped His disciple's attack and healed the soldier's ear. Then Jesus asked the soldiers whom they were looking for, and they replied, "Jesus of Nazareth." He answered, "I am He."

It was hard to see in the black night, but it was not hard to hear. They could hardly believe their ears. Here was the man whom the priest had told them was dangerous and an enemy of Rome. He didn't look dangerous, and He certainly was different from any other enemy. But it is hard to tell when you have such poor light. The torches were burning down and the lanterns were dim. One of His own disciples, Judas, had turned Him in, and the priests said He was dangerous. So the soldiers did what they were told to do and arrested this man called Jesus.

I have a drawing of a lantern that will help you remember the story of how and where Jesus was arrested. I want you to keep this in a special place so that you will never forget how that night began.

God bless you. Amen.

The Rope

So the soldiers, their officer, and the Jewish police arrested Jesus and bound him. First they took him to Annas, who was the father-in-law of Caiaphas, the high priest that year.
— John 18:12-13

Object: A rope

Do you remember where we left our story last week? Do you remember that the soldiers had arrested Jesus in the olive grove when it was late at night, and the only light they had was a lantern to see by? If you remember that, then you will know right where our story begins today.

Jesus was thought to be a dangerous man because he had chased all of the robbers and greedy people out of the Temple. The priests and Pharisees thought He was dangerous because He taught new things about God that they didn't know and were afraid to learn. They were afraid that the people would listen to Jesus instead of to them. That made them afraid and angry.

The soldiers were told that He was dangerous, and they did not want to take any chances. He did not look like a dangerous man who would hurt anyone, but when you are a soldier, you are trained to follow orders. Their orders were to arrest Him and bring Him to the house of Annas, the Chief Priest.

The soldiers did with Jesus what they always did with some-one they arrested. They tied Him up. Jesus was told to put His hands behind Him, and one of the soldiers took a strong rope and bound His hands. A rope can burn your wrists if it is tight. It cuts right through the skin. Jesus felt the soldier jerk the rope to pull it tight and then knot it in place.

Out of the garden the soldiers came with their captive be-tween them. Back down the hill and across the Kidron Valley they went until they came to the giant wall that surrounded the city of Jerusalem. The sentries who were posted at the huge gates swung them open and allowed the soldiers and their prisoner to pass through. It had been only a few days before that when Jesus had ridden through the same streets on the back of a donkey colt and had heard the cheers of the people who lived in this city. Now He was led like a criminal to the house of the chief priest, Annas. It is hard to walk well when your hands are tied behind you, and I suppose that Jesus got a few commands like, "Hurry up" and "Watch where you are going." But Jesus never said a smart thing back. He went because He knew that the soldiers were doing what they were told to do and what they thought was right.

The soldiers took Him into the house of Annas. Remem-ber that it was still dark outside, but when they came into the room it was like entering the house of a king. There sat An-nas looking down on Jesus as if He were something dirty. He asked Jesus about His disciple friends and what He had taught them. Jesus told the chief priests that He taught them the same thing that He taught in the temple. All of the Jewish leaders had heard Him teach, and many of them were present that night in Annas' house. One of the soldiers who liked to be a bully grabbed Jesus who was still tied with the rope, hit Him in the face with his fist and screamed, "Is that the way to an-swer the High Priest?"

Jesus looked at the soldier and said to him, "If I lied, prove it. Should you hit a man for telling the truth?"

Annas knew what Jesus taught. He had heard people talk about Jesus and the things He said and the good things He did. How do you punish a man for doing good and teaching love? It was a hard question, and one that Annas found hard to answer. But still he hated Him because the people loved Jesus instead of him. Somehow Annas had to get rid of Jesus or he would lose his position and power.

But Annas knew that he was not the only one who was in trouble. Maybe someone else could do what he did not want to do. So Annas told the soldier to take away the man tied with a rope to his son-in-law, Caiaphas. Maybe he would find the words to make Jesus look bad and the Jewish leaders look good. Jesus stood, hands tied, listening to the threats and questions of the chief priest. His courage never lessened even when the soldier hit Him in the face. Jesus knew that God was with Him and that everything would be made right in the end.

I have a picture of a rope for you to keep to help you remember the night that Jesus went to the chief priest's house and kept His courage. I hope that this sign will give you courage also.

God bless you. Amen.

The Crown
Of Thorns

And after flogging Jesus, he handed him over to be crucified.
Then the soldiers of the governor took Jesus into the gover-
nor's headquarters, and they gathered the whole cohort around
him. They stripped him and put a scarlet robe on him, and
after twisting some thorns into a crown, they put it on his head.
They put a reed in his right hand and knelt before him and
mocked him, saying, "Hail, King of the Jews!" They spat on
him, and took the reed and struck him on the head.
— Matthew 27:26b-30

Object: A crown of thorns

_____

Good morning, boys and girls. Perhaps you will remember where we left off last week with our story, but let me tell
you a little bit about what has happened to Jesus since we left
Him being taken out of Annas' house and over to the house
of Caiaphas, another Jewish leader. Jesus had been shoved
and pushed around from one place to another. He even spent
a little time in the palace of Herod, a kind of Jewish king who
worked for the Romans. All of these people were afraid to
do anything. They knew what the people thought about Jesus
and how much they loved Him; but they were also very sure
that if they did not do something, the people would begin to
follow Jesus rather than them. It was a terrible problem for

13

the Jewish leaders. The only thing they could do was to get the Roman Governor, Pilate, to work with them and do to Jesus what they were afraid to do.

Pilate had a boss, too, and his name was Caesar. He was the most powerful ruler on earth. Caesar did not like any trouble in the places that he ruled, and he told his governors so. Their job was to keep the peace, see that the taxes were collected and the Roman law enforced.

Pilate knew that he could not have any trouble with the Jewish leaders. When Jesus was sent to Pilate, he suddenly wished that he was not the governor. Here was an honest man whom people loved and the leaders hated. He would have problems no matter what he did. He tried to get Jesus to say that He was wrong and to apologize, but of course Jesus would not do that. He finally gave up trying to change the mind of Jesus and gave Him back to the soldiers before crucifying Him.

The soldiers knew now that Jesus was going to die, and some of them were cruel men. They had a little game that they played with men who were going to die, and they took Jesus down into an area to play it with him. The game was called the "Game of Kings." Since many people believed that Jesus was the Messiah, the King of the Jews, the soldiers could hardly wait to play. There was only one difference. Jesus really was a King, but they did not know it. They took off His clothes and beat Him with a very harsh whip, and then while He was bleeding they put a scarlet red robe over him and a reed in his hand and pretended it was a royal scepter. Then the cruelest thing of all was when a soldier made a crown from a thorn branch and shoved it down on Jesus' head and began to chant, "Hail, King of the Jews. Hail, King of the Jews." Jesus, standing in the middle, was helpless while a group of soldiers made fun of Him with very cruel punishment. While He was bleeding and being tortured, He prayed to God for strength and courage. Jesus received what He asked for, and the soldiers could not get Him to break down and cry or ask for mercy. He stood there and forgave the soldiers for their evil and prayed for God to help Him.

When the soldiers had done everything they could think of, they took off the robe and put His own clothing back on His blood-stained back. They took away the scepter, but they left the crown of thorns on His head and marched Him back up the stairs and out to the crowd. He didn't look like the same man who had stood before the Governor only hours before, but He was even more determined to do what God asked of Him now than He was before.

The crowd was led by the Jewish leaders who chanted, "Crucify Him, crucify Him, crucify Him." It was terrible, but that is what happened. Jesus was led away to a hill called Calvary. On the way He carried a cross. Imagine what He must have looked like, bent over, bleeding through his clothes, and carrying that cross. But on top of His head was a crown, a crown of thorns.

I have a picture of a crown of thorns today to help you remember what happened to Jesus. The soldiers played with Him, mocked Him and even spit on Him. But even the crown of thorns is a sign for us that teaches us how much Jesus loves and forgives, even those who hate Him.

God bless you. Amen.

The Dice
And The Robe

*When the soldiers had crucified Jesus, they took his clothes
and divided them into four parts, one for each soldier. They
also took his tunic; now the tunic was seamless, woven in one
piece from the top. So they said to one another, "Let us not
tear it, but cast lots for it to see who will get it." This was
to fulfill what the scripture says, "They divided my clothes
among themselves, and for my clothing they cast lots."*
— John 19:23-24

Object: Dice and a robe

You will remember that Jesus was beaten and given a crown
of thorns to wear in our last story. The very end of the story
told us that the soldiers led Jesus up a hill called Calvary to
be crucified. It was a hard walk since they made Jesus walk
back and forth and up and down the streets to warn other people about what could happen to them if they acted or did anything like Jesus did. This is what they did with everyone who
was crucified.

At the top of the hill there was a place where a hole had
been dug for the bottom part of the cross. They took off Jesus'
clothes and put them in a pile, then they nailed Jesus to the
cross. You can imagine how much Jesus must have hurt when
this happened. But He stood the pain. The cross was lifted

high in the air with Jesus on it so that everyone could see Him. It was a terrible way to die. The people who knew and loved Jesus were crushed. They cried and screamed, but mostly they just stood and prayed for God to give Jesus strength.

The soldiers were different from the other people. They had seen lots of men die and many of them crucified. They knew this was their job, and they tried not to listen to the cries and screams of Jesus' friends.

One of the things that the soldiers did get at the time of the crucifixion was the clothes of the man who was put to death on the cross. The soldiers seemed to like the idea that they got something for nothing. The Bible tells us that the soldiers divided Jesus' clothes into four piles, one for each of them. Since His robe was seamless, it was considered more valuable, so they decided to gamble for it. They would roll some dice, and the man with the highest number would keep it. There was Jesus dying on the cross with nails through His hands and feet, and the soldiers were gambling and playing games for His robe. It doesn't sound real, but that is what happened. Jesus is praying; the soldiers are playing.

We don't know which soldier won Jesus' robe or anything else about it, but it is something to think about. Yet, we think that Jesus knew what was going to happen because the scriptures of the Old Testament had said that this was going to happen. It was one more time that a person could remember that the death of Jesus was according to a great plan that was made by God.

Above His head was a sign that had been made by Pilate which read, "Jesus of Nazareth, King of the Jews." Around Him were many of the people who had followed and loved Him. But also at the foot of the cross were some men who were trying to forget that Jesus was even there. Jesus thought of his mother Mary at the foot of the cross and asked His disciple John to take care of her. He remembered another man who was being crucified that day not too far from Him, and He forgave his sins and promised him a place to live with God forever. He remembered that He was dying so that everyone could live forever with God. He even remembered to forgive the soldiers who did not know what they were doing to the Son of God.

That is why I have this picture of some dice and a robe for you. It is to help you remember Jesus and the love that He has for you. Some people try to forget Jesus so that they can have things for nothing or things that they should not have. You and I have that kind of a problem when we wish that God did not know what we were doing or thinking. You and I will remember Jesus and the way that He was crucified that day in Jerusalem.

God bless you. Amen.

The Ladder
And The Sponge

From noon on, darkness came over the whole land until three in the afternoon. And about three o'clock Jesus cried with a loud voice, "Eli, Eli, lema sabachthani," that is, "My God, my God, why have you forsaken me?" When some of the bystanders heard it, they said, "This man is calling for Elijah." At once one of them ran and got a sponge, filled it with sour wine, put it on a stick, and gave it to him to drink. But the others said, "Wait, let us see whether Elijah will come to save him."

— Matthew 27:45-49

Object: A ladder and a sponge

We left our story last week with Jesus hanging on the cross and the Roman soldiers playing games with dice for His clothes. It was a horrible afternoon in Jerusalem. The Bible tells us that at noon, when the sun is usually at its brightest, there was nothing but darkness. It looked like it was night time, and there was a big storm coming. The people who stood around the cross were cold and crying since the people they loved were dying on crosses. The soldiers watched the people to make sure that none of them tried to rescue Jesus or the other two criminals who were being crucified that day.

The pain of standing on a nail driven through His feet was terrible for Jesus, and His arms were tired from being held outstretched with the nails. But there was nothing He could do except look to His Father in Heaven and pray for new strength. One of the criminals was yelling at Jesus to save them if He was the Son of God. "If you have that kind of power why don't you use it?" he screamed at Jesus. The other thief felt something different about Him and told the screaming thief to be quiet.

The pain was unbelievable, and Jesus began to sweat drops of blood where the crown of thorns bit into His head. His throat was dry and He had to make a major effort even to breathe. Still, He looked out with love in His eyes for all of the people, including the ones who tormented Him, with words like, "If you are the Son of God save yourself, come down from the cross." When He did nothing they laughed at Him. None of the followers of Jesus laughed but instead they prayed for death to come quickly so that Jesus would not have to suffer long.

Once when everything seemed quiet and the soldiers were watching some black clouds move toward the hill on which they were standing, Jesus let out a yell in Hebrew that sounded like this, "Eli, Eli, lema sabachthani." It scared the soldiers to see someone so near to death be able to shout in such a loud voice. Some of the people who were not paying attention very closely thought that Jesus was calling for Elijah. What Jesus had said was, "My God, my God, why have you forsaken me?" Those who heard Him felt awful. If Jesus felt that God had given up on Him, then what was left? It was for His Father that He did what He did. Did Jesus feel that God had really left Him to die all alone? Later, when men had a chance to think, they remembered that these were words from a Psalm. Jesus knew what it felt like to be a man, filled with sin. He knew how we feel when we have sinned and God seems so far away.

One of the soldiers ran over to Jesus with a stick with a sponge on the end, and climbed a ladder. He took the sponge and put it to Jesus' dry lips. The sponge was filled with sour wine or vinegar and it tasted terrible. But now it was for something else. It made His dry lips and throat feel better, and it was supposed to help kill the pain. At least one of the soldiers was beginning to feel something different for Jesus.

But the other people who were not followers of Him and the other soldiers began yelling at this one who tried to help. "Let him alone," they shouted. "Let's see if Elijah comes and saves him." Then all of these people let out a big laugh since they knew that Elijah had been dead for hundreds of years. The soldier came down from the ladder, but he could not take his eyes off Jesus. Even with all His pain and sorrow, the soldier could see that Jesus was filled with love and forgiveness for those who hated Him.

I have a small picture of that ladder and sponge for you. I hope that you will keep it somewhere so you can remember the day that Jesus felt all of our sin and the sins of the whole world crush Him. You will also remember how one soldier began to think a little differently about Jesus and tried to tell Him that he was sorry. Maybe when you think of the soldier you will remember to tell Jesus that you are sorry for your sins.

The Spear

Since it was the day of Preparation, the Jews did not want the bodies left on the cross during the sabbath, especially because that sabbath was a day of great solemnity. So they asked Pilate to have the legs of the crucified men broken and the bodies removed. Then the soldiers came and broke the legs of the first and of the other who had been crucified with him. But when they came to Jesus and saw that he was already dead, they did not break his legs. Instead, one of the soldiers pierced his side with a spear, and at once blood and water came out. (He who saw this has testified so that you also may believe. His testimony is true, and he knows that he tells the truth.)
— *John 19:31-35*

Object: A spear

Perhaps you remember the moment that we spoke of when the soldier came up to Jesus, climbed the ladder and put a sponge with sour wine to Jesus' lips. Jesus died very shortly after that moment. I don't know how many people who were there that day heard Jesus say it, but after the soldier lifted the sponge to His lips Jesus said, "It is finished." He was dead. It seemed impossible that only a few hours before He was eating with His disciples and now He was dead.

This was a Friday and only a few hours away from the Sabbath which was the Jewish holy day, like our Sunday. The

Jewish leaders didn't want any sign of a dead body or any sort of trouble showing on the Sabbath, so they asked the Roman Governor, Pilate, to have the legs of the men who were still on the cross broken so that they would die sooner. Not only were they beaten and nailed to the crosses, but now they were going to break the legs of the crucified.

The soldiers didn't mind. At least most of them didn't care, because they thought this was part of their job. The two thieves who were on crosses with Jesus were not dead, and when the soldiers came to their crosses they struck them several times across their legs until they were sure that their legs were broken. How cruel, how terribly cruel.

But when they came to Jesus they stopped and looked at him carefully. They could see no sign of breath or any other movement. He was dead. There was no need to break His legs. He was not going anywhere. For a moment it seemed as if they were not going to do anything, just pass Him by. But just as the last soldier had taken a step away from Jesus, he stopped and turned, and then he lifted his spear and shoved it into the side of Jesus. As the spear pierced the skin there was a rush of water and blood that covered the point and rushed down the handle. There was no sound, no moan, and the soldiers were satisfied that the one with the sign "King of the Jews" was really dead.

The soldier pulled back his spear and joined the other soldiers who were walking ahead. The friends of Jesus were now also very sure that Jesus was dead. They could think about all the things that He had said and the healings that He had performed, but they could never again talk with Him or share a laugh, or a piece of bread. Jesus was dead and there was no doubt about it.

In a little while a man named Joseph, who was a secret disciple of Jesus and also part of the Jewish leadership, went to the Roman Governor, Pilate, and very boldly asked if he could have permission to bury Jesus in his tomb. Pilate agreed and told him to go ahead and do with Jesus what he wanted. Another secret disciple by the name of Nicodemus asked if he could help Joseph, and when told that he could, he brought a hundred pounds of special ointment and spices to cover the body of Jesus before burial.

With those arrangements made and the time drawing close to the beginning of the Sabbath, Joseph and Nicodemus moved quickly to the tomb in the garden. They wrapped His body in a long linen cloth bathed in the ointment and spices. When that was finished they left quickly but with great sadness in their hearts. As they went out of the tomb there were some soldiers coming to take their place as the guard. A heavy stone was rolled in front of the tomb to shut it off. It was a stone of such great weight that not even several men could move it.

A spear had been the final proof that Jesus was dead. No one could live with a wound like that in his side. Jesus the Christ would never be the same again. I have a small picture of that spear for you to keep and remember the day that Jesus died. The soldier who threw it into His side never knew that he was piercing the side of the Son of God, but some day it would serve as proof to a disciple that Jesus lived again. Remember that even as He died, He did so with a prayer on His lips. He forgave everyone who had sinned against God and Him. Now we should be ready to do the same.

God bless you. Amen.

The Empty Tomb

And suddenly there was a great earthquake; for an angel of the Lord, descending from heaven, came and rolled back the stone and sat on it. His appearance was like lightning, and his clothing white as snow. For fear of him the guards shook and became like dead men. But the angel said to the women, "Do not be afraid; I know that you are looking for Jesus who was crucified. He is not here; for he has been raised, as he said. Come, see the place where he lay."

— Matthew 28:2-6

Object: A picture of an empty tomb

Good morning, boys and girls. Today is Easter Sunday, a very special day. I will tell you why it is special, but first, do you remember where we left off with our story of Jesus last week? It was a Friday night, just before the Jewish Sabbath, when Joseph of Arimathea and a friend named Nicodemus wrapped the dead body of Jesus in linen and some spices and buried Him in the tomb. It was a terrible day, that Friday, for all of the followers of Jesus. They could hardly believe that this good man had been killed for the wonderful things that He had done. But He was dead and there was nothing that they could do but feel sorry.

Some of the women who had loved Jesus, like His mother and some other very close friends, wanted to do the kind of

25

things that they felt should be done for a dead person, so they made plans to go to the tomb on Sunday morning. They got up very early, before the sunrise, and began to walk to the tomb. On the way they talked about the problems that they would have with the big stone in front of the tomb. They knew that they could not move it, and unless they had some kind of help their trip would be worthless. Still, they wanted to go, and if nothing else just sit outside the tomb and pray where they could feel closer to Jesus. It seemed like the least that they could do.

While they were walking toward the place of the tomb there was a terrible shaking of the earth. The trees shook, rocks rolled, and large cracks appeared in the ground.

At the tomb there were some other things happening. While the earthquake was going on, an angel came down from heaven and pushed the stone away from the entrance to the tomb and then just sat on top of it. He was dressed all in white and his face was as bright as the sunshine. The soldiers were shocked. No one man could move that stone. And what about the looks of this person? No one looked like that. The soldiers were so amazed that they fainted. These were the same soldiers who beat up Jesus, spit on Him, made a crown of thorns, hung Him on a cross and even threw a spear through Him. But now, seeing an angel for the first time caused them to faint.

They were still lying on the ground when the women came and saw that the big stone had been rolled away. How glad they were, but what had happened to Jesus? Was He gone or was He still inside?

Before they could look for themselves the angel spoke and told them not to be afraid. He said, "I know you are looking for Jesus, who was crucified, but He isn't here! For He has come back to life again, just as He said He would. Come in and see where His body was lying." They went in. Jesus was gone. There was no body. There was nothing but the cloth that was folded into the shape of a triangle and big enough to cover the face. That was all there was in the tomb.

The women were frightened. The angel was smiling and the soldiers were still lying on the ground in a faint. The angel told the women to go and tell the disciples of Jesus what they had seen and to tell them that Jesus would meet them in Galilee. The women ran away as fast as they could. They were frightened but happy, so very, very happy.

As they were running toward town to tell the disciples what the angel had said, they almost ran into a person who was standing in front of them. It was Jesus, and they fell to the ground and kissed His feet and told Him how glad they were to see Him. Jesus told them to go on ahead and to do as the angel had told them. They jumped to their feet and ran on ahead.

Meanwhile some of the soldiers had awakened and when they found the tomb empty, and the angel gone, they ran to the Temple to tell what had happened.

The Jewish leaders did not know what to do. They finally agreed that they had to have a different story, so they promised the soldiers some money if they would only tell everyone that the disciples of Jesus had stolen the body while they were asleep. The soldiers finally agreed if the priests promised to stick up for them when the governor questioned them. That was the final agreement made between the Jewish leaders and the soldiers. But for Christians, the real story is the one that happened on that first Easter Sunday.

I have something for you to remember it by on this Easter Day. It is a picture of that empty tomb. I want you to take it and keep it where you will always remember the day that Jesus came back to life from the dead. It is important to remember because Jesus promises us that we will share the same promise of new life with him some day.

God bless you. Amen.